CARE

Alexander Zeldin

methuen | drama
LONDON • NEW YORK • OXFORD • NEW DELHI • SYDNEY

METHUEN DRAMA
Bloomsbury Publishing Plc, 50 Bedford Square, London, WC1B 3DP, UK
Bloomsbury Publishing Inc, 1359 Broadway, New York, NY 10018, USA
Bloomsbury Publishing Ireland, 29 Earlsfort Terrace, Dublin 2, D02 AY28, Ireland

BLOOMSBURY, METHUEN DRAMA and the Methuen Drama logo are trademarks of Bloomsbury Publishing Plc

First published in 2026 by Methuen Drama

Cover design by Megan Wilson
Cover image *Mutter mit Zwillingen* by Kaethe Kollwitz via Wikimedia

A catalogue record for this book is available from the British Library.

A catalog record for this book is available from the Library of Congress.

ISBN: PB: 978-1-3506-4637-7
ePDF: 978-1-3506-4638-4
eBook: 978-1-3506-4639-1

Series: Modern Plays

Typeset by Jones Ltd, London

For product safety related questions contact productsafety@bloomsbury.com.

To find out more about our authors and books visit www.bloomsbury.com and sign up for our newsletters.

A Young Vic and A Zeldin Company co-production

CARE

Written and directed by Alexander Zeldin

CARE

Written and directed by Alexander Zeldin.

CARE is translated and adapted from Alexander Zeldin's play *Une Mort Dans La Famille*, which was first performed at Ateliers Berthiers on 4 February 2022, produced by Odéon-Théâtre de l'Europe.

Creative Team

Alexander Zeldin	Writer and Director
Rosanna Vize	Set Designer
Natasha Jenkins	Costume Designer
James Farncombe	Lighting Designer
Josh Anio Grigg	Sound Designer
Marcin Rudy	Movement Director
Jacob Sparrow	Casting Director
Katharine Hardman	Intimacy Director
Sam Lyon-Behan	Fight Director
Carol Fairlamb	Voice Coach
Faye Merralls	Dramaturg
Patricia Ojehonmon	Dramatherapist
Caroline McCall	Costume Supervisor
Laura Flowers	Props Supervisor
Kaleya Baxe	Associate Director
Emma Kopf	Trainee Assistant Director
Sara Mackenzie	Assistant Costume Supervisor
Lucy Horton	Wigs, Hair and Make Up Consultant

Cast

Linda Bassett	Joan
Hayley Carmichael	Simone
Rosie Cavaliero	Lynn
Taru Devani	Aditi

Richard Durden	John
Aoife Gaston	Fanta
Llewella Gideon	Hazel
William Lawlor	Laurie
Ethan Mahony	Robbie
Ann Mitchell	Agnes
Diana Payan	Paula
Winston Sookhan	Eugene
Charlie Webb	Robbie

Production & Stage Management Team

Hannah Blamire	Production Manager
Pippa Meyer	Company Stage Manager
Amy Steadman	Company Stage Manager
Hannah Gillett	Deputy Stage Manager
Grace Hans	Assistant Stage Manager (Book Cover)
Bronte MacInnes	Assistant Stage Manager
Shelia Manson	Chaperone
Zoe Kennedy-Lamb	Chaperone

About the Young Vic

Founded in 1970 as a space for world-premiere productions and unexpected takes on classic plays, the Young Vic has been one of London's leading theatres for more than fifty years.

Welcoming 100,000 visitors a year, the Young Vic stands out in the nation's cultural landscape for balancing daring commercial drive and artistic flair with genuine grassroots social impact work within our community. This success is seen most vividly in the audience group for which we are famous; the most diverse, lively and engaged in London. This is the fruit of years of building involvement among local young people. We forge deep connections in our neighbourhood through our Taking Part programme, where we engage with over 15,000 people every year via a wide range of projects, from skills-based workshops to on-stage performances.

We believe great art belongs to everyone. Ticket prices are kept low no matter how high the demand and 10% of tickets are given free within the local community, enabling a unique, no-risk taste of great theatre for thousands of people.

Our unique, fully-flexible auditoria allows us to present great plays by and with the next generation of theatre artists alongside work by some of the world's great directors, actors and designers. We are proud to be a Director's Theatre known for launching careers and a combination of youth and genius which makes us one of the most vibrant theatres in the UK.

Built upon the principles of access, innovation and community, the Young Vic is deepening its roots nationally and internationally. Recent transfers include *Punch, Best of Enemies* and *Oklahoma!* in the West End and *Death of a Salesman* and *The Collaboration* on Broadway.

Some theatres present great plays. Some give young artists opportunities to grow. Some build strong and lasting relationships with their community. The Young Vic does all three.

Artistic Director	**Nadia Fall**
Executive Director	**Lucy Pattison**

Youngvic.org

THE SEASON CIRCLE

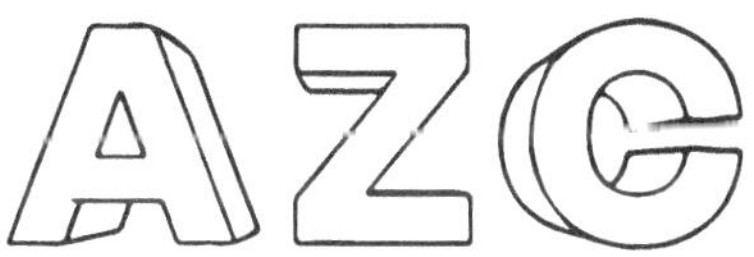

***A Zeldin Company** was founded in 2019 to develop and produce the plays of Alexander Zeldin and tour them internationally. Under the co-directorship of Alexander Zeldin and producer Faye Merralls, the company toured to twenty-five cities across thirteen countries in just four years. As well as visiting the leading international arts festivals in Paris, Avignon, Athens, Rome and Vienna, AZC has presented work with the Park Avenue Armory in New York where Zeldin's play LOVE received seven Drama Desk Award nominations. In 2022, Zeldin set up Compagnie A Zeldin France.*

CARE

Alexander Zeldin

To my mother and my brother

Joan Taylor the grandmother, eighties
Lynn Sadetzki the mother, fifties
Laurie Sadetzki sixteen, elder son
Robbie Sadetzki twelve, younger son

Hazel Smith (care worker)
Fanta Keita (care worker)

Simone Simmons (resident)
John Francis (resident)
Paula Farr (resident)
Agnes Bailey (resident)
Aditi Parekh (resident)
Eugene Samba (resident)

Other residents of the care home.

notes:

A '.' on its own means a thought that doesn't become a word.

A '/' indicates where the next speaker should come in.

Text in (brackets) indicates a thought where it might not be clear.

Act One

Scene One

March

The Common Room of The Cedars Care Home. It is perhaps a converted school, or in any case a building that has been repurposed. Upstage right, there is a double door that clearly leads out to the street, on which there is a code system, a lock. A loud buzz sound indicates that someone is at the door. Upstage right, there is a door leading to a disabled toilet, and then, SR of that, a corridor that goes off to the rest of the home, through which the residents are wheeled. Perhaps some art is on the walls. Some prints of paintings, fading at the edges in their frames, a noticeboard, with some photos of staff and residents. The walls, likely stud walls, have places where they have been hastily cleaned with a magic sponge, leaving traces.

Downstage, there is some by now quite tired furniture, with easily wipeable surfaces, and cushions with once lively patterns, now faded. The floor has seen better days too, a kind of brown, fake resin floor, the type seen occasionally in school gyms or administrative buildings of bygone years in England. Above, the lights, a row of fluorescent tubes, occasionally flicker, betraying a complication with the power source. As the building faces south, through its windows, which, although unseen, are to be imagined in the stalls, the light of day comes shining in, creating occasional shadows on the back wall and the floor, the furniture, depending on the time of day, and the movement of the clouds above: a shadow play as the light passes through on its way to the night time, when darkness enters, but the stars can be seen.

Aditi *(100 years old) is sitting or wandering a little as the audience comes in. She occasionally looks at them, but she's muttering under her breath. This lasts a while. She should be in a wheelchair or a walker. In any case, clearly needing help.*

She should be holding a call button . . . maybe she's saying 'help help' at a barely audible volume.

Paula *enters. There is no interaction between* **Paula** *and* **Aditi**.

Paula *exits, as if she's forgotten something.*

Joan *is brought into the room by* **Hazel**, *she is in a wheelchair.*

Hazel It won't be long now

Beat.

Joan Where are my family

Aditi I need the bathroom.

Hazel *(to* **Aditi***)* I'll be right there

Aditi My hanky. I lost my hankie!

Hazel I'll get you another

Aditi *is becoming more animated.*

Aditi HELP! HELP! Bathroom! Bathroom!

Hazel There's a bit of a wait for the bathroom this morning.

Hazel *is already moving back out of the room.*

For a moment the two women are left alone on stage. **Aditi** *goes on muttering to herself.* **Joan** *looks ahead of herself, but then, almost as if she's afraid and with some considerable effort she glances at* **Aditi** *and with some trepidation smiles at her. She speaks quite softly.*

As a general note in what follows, residents stare in front of themselves, and are very much in their own worlds, their own reality, only intermittently engaging with each other in direct connection and conversation.

Beat, **Joan** *thinks about it, nods, as if to say hello, maybe mumbles hello, an effort to connect.*

Fanta *enters, at speed, and begins to arrange some of the larger chairs and tables around.*

Paula *is brought back in by* **Hazel**. **Paula** *is brandishing her walking stick and shaking it aggressively towards people.*

Paula RETREAT / RETREAT

Hazel *(dodging what seems like a punch)* Hey!

Alright.

Paula *makes her way slowly over. Pointing to where* **Aditi** *is sat.*

Paula I sit there.

Aditi *mumbles to herself.*

Enter, **Agnes** *(90s), dressed with elegance. She commits to what she says and speaks quite loudly, but at first with no clear addressee.*

Agnes Yes.

Fanta I'll get you / another

Paula It's MY chair.

Agnes Yes

Paula It's my chair.

Hazel Yeh? Well you'll get to sit on it tomorrow /

Fanta *rushes out again. For a few beats they are left alone, mumbling, occasionally, so that there is never a complete silence.* **Agnes** *has been in the room for a few beats.* **Hazel** *attends to something off and then re-enters.*

To **Joan***:*

Agnes good morning. Yes.

Paula my chair.

Agnes Yes. Ah!

Re-enter **Hazel**.

Paula .

Meanwhile, **Aditi***, still absorbed in her lost handkerchief, is crying.* **Aditi** *and* **Hazel** *speak their next lines as they exit to the bathroom together*

Aditi I need the bathroom / the bathroom and my hankie my hankie

Hazel come on come on let's not be crying now Aditi?

She takes **Aditi** *to the bathroom; as they exit,* **Aditi** *continues to whimper.*

Pause.

Paula Are you Helena?

Joan No.

Who is Helena

Paula .

Fanta *comes back in with* **Eugene** *following her.*

Agnes Are we going to / sing or not . . .

Paula *(leaning over to* **Joan***)* Do you know the way home.

Enter **Simone***, unaccompanied, loud, dishevelled and only wearing one shoe.* **Agnes** *looks at her, glares at her more like.* **Simone** *looks at* **Joan**.

Simone Fresh blood?

Fanta Who wants a nice hot Coffee? Tea? Hot Chocolate?

They all answer together.

Paula/Simone Coffee

Agnes Hot Chocolate.

She looks over to **Eugene** *who is in his own world;* **Fanta** *is already rushed off her feet making the coffee.*

Fanta Eugene?

Re-enter **Hazel** *without* **Aditi** *who is still in the toilet.*

Hazel No no she can't have coffee!

Fanta Oh I'm sorry.

Hazel you need to really look at the charts not just give them anything

Fanta I'm so sorry

Hazel it's OK, you just drink it.

So, hello, everyone /

Agnes let us get started because this is dragging /

Paula you're talking about me! Who said Mrs Farr!

Hazel OK but hang on, Agnes . . . I've brought you all down because I'd like to introduce you all to Joan? She arrived last night.

Joan oh . . . / look, really there is no need.

Hazel Come on everyone, say hello.

A couple of 'hellos' emerge. Once **Fanta** *finishes making and delivering the teas/coffees, she exits.*

Simone I'm quite happy to talk but y / you gotta talk?

Joan I?

Simone / she doesn't (want to)

Hazel Joan, why don't you say a few words to introduce yourself then we'll do the activity?

A pause. Some residents look at **Joan**.

Joan oh no, there's no need . . . I'm only here for a short time just a few weeks of . . . respite care. I had a nasty fall but I'm fine, I'm fine not . . . in the same predicament /

Agnes SPEAK up, Madam

Joan don't take any trouble over me.

Beat, **Simone** *laughs and under her breath says 'Yeh, right'.*

Joan I'm actually waiting for my daughter – / she's coming to get me.

Hazel But you came from the coast, to live with your daughter, didn't you! People love hearing about life stories.

Joan Oh, yes . . .

She laughs a little, as if to dismiss, but somehow this falls flat.

Hazel You had a lovely life by the seaside, didn't you?

Joan Yes, with my husband

Hazel Yeh? Who likes the seaside? Let's open it up, come on, let's have a discussion activity

Fanta *enters and* **Hazel** *signals to her to go and get* **Aditi** *from the toilet*

Beat.

Paula Nothing wrong with the seaside.

Pause. **Joan** *sees that* **Hazel** *wants her to talk.*

Hazel Come on, Joan!

Joan Well, I have two grandchildren

Robbie is twelve. The older one, Laurie is . . .

Paula I have three granddaughters.

Five daughters.

General 'ooh's, 'ahh's from the assembled people.

A lot of women, no no.

Joan The other one is sixteen.

he's caused a lot of trouble for his mother . . .

I live with my daughter, I'm not staying.

Agnes, *during this, looks around the room, lost.*

Beat.

Hazel And how long have you lived here?

Agnes Is your daughter here too

Agnes *looks around.*

Joan I've been there about two years. The boys lost their father.

That's the story. He died suddenly.

Hazel Oh no / . . .

Joan Yes, he was ill. I came to help.

Paula What was / lost.

Agnes I lost it.

Enter **Fanta** *with* **Aditi**

Joan My daughter is not a very strong person.

Agnes In the war /

Hazel Oh isn't she? What does she do

Joan she sort of teaches English, literacy really, to people who aren't . . . Refugees and so on

Hazel Oh wow

Fanta wow

Beat.

Agnes The war is over. It's over. Long ago

Paula Because if we're talking about what was lost /

Agnes *(upset)* A LOT was lost. A lot.

Beat.

Paula Sorry is this mobility and creativity?

Simone Yeh I know! Mobility and creativity. I want to sing. I'll sing

She begins to sing, and is interrupted by **Agnes**.

'lala la / fuckeroo, fuckeroo! Dos Gardenias! Dos Gardenias!'

Agnes you call that singing? you're shouting and crying in the street bothering everyone . . . My husband will shut you up / when gets back from hospital.

Simone Shut up

Agnes STOP / it

Simone shut up. I said.

Agnes *looks over to* **Joan**

Agnes you know she she she was a lady of the night, / so they say

This comment draws some laughter, some reactions from the wider group.

Hazel Agnes

Come on now. Let's be nice.

Simone Fuck you.

Hazel SIMONE! Please.

Who here has travelled? Who's been overseas?

Simone DO you know how much it costs to go to the beach.

Enter **John** – **Fanta** *is holding his hand.*

Fanta Mr Francis will have been overseas . . .

Agnes Elocution.

Aditi / mummy . . .

Simone You need a buck / et, spades.

Paula Too late, too / late too late too late.

Hazel Mr Francis, John, was a big shot / businessman. He went everywhere

Simone Big shot

Agnes But his family are cheap / so here he is

Aditi Mummy . . .

Simone Ice cream.

Paula Too late.

Hazel HOW ARE YOU TODAY?

John *is distracted as if he's not fully in the conversation.*

John Good morning . . . sir.

Hazel You travelled?

John I don't know.

He's not letting go of **Fanta**.

Fanta yeh that's my hand

Hazel Yes, let her go . . . come on . . . that's right Fanta is still training and, well. Fresh. Be nice

Agnes Is she a temp because / they are helpless.

Fanta No no! I'm full time.

Simone Fanta Lemon haha /

John *lets go of* **Fanta***'s hand and smiles.*

Hazel probation.

Fanta Sorry.

Hazel We were talking about travel

Because Joan is new and we're doing an activity meeting her.

She lived by the sea.

John Good girl. Don't let them mess you around.

Beat.

Paula I haven't been anywhere. (*Proudly.*) I never left the UK.

Hazel OK . . .

Paula People left the city on horseback

Simone All these sick / people what are we doing here

Short beat.

Paula I have four daughters.

no, no . . . five.

Hazel thank you, Paula

From here on in, it is clear that **Joan** *is trying to manoeuvre her way out.*

Joan excuse me

John Well depends (miss) . . . on how you look at things /

Simone Well you look DONE FOR.

John *smiles, as if he hasn't quite understood.*

John no but when it comes to travel . . . there are people that go to one place . . .

Paula NOTHING WRONG WITH THE UK. What's the point? Of going anywhere / I always said.

Hazel yes? One place?

John one place yes . . . and now people go to many places they go to a country and they don't know why they / are going . . .

Hazel interesting

Simone I always dent where I want . . .

John *looks up, with a childlike expression on his face.*

John No but / there are places, that have . . .

Simone I've been all the palaces of the kingdom
I'VE SLEPT IN FANTASTIC BEDS with FANTASTIC MEN

Joan Oh god . . .

John . . .

Significance? /

He smiles as if he has some sense of mystery.

Significance.

Hazel Yes, some places should have significance . . .

Like the beach . . .

John Or . . . the forest, behind.

He looks over at **Joan**.

Joan I enjoy the sea. / Yes

John At school. What dreams?

Hazel OK! Great I'm loving this conversation! Isn't this great?

Beat.

Joan? The sea?

Joan Everyone enjoys the sea. I lived by the sea I could hear it.

I am not very talkative.

I'm sorry.

Pause.

Aditi I'm going to South Africa.

Hazel That's great.

Aditi My mummy is there.

Agnes I have lived all over the world so there is nothing surprising in any of this

Fanta AH!!! No way.

Hazel Yes that's right, you did Ag / nes

Agnes I did with my husband. We spent many years in the Kenya, actually.

Hazel *and* **Fanta** *share a look about* **Agnes**' *husband.*

Fanta That's AMAZING. Tell us your story?

Throughout the following **Eugene** *– who has just been sitting in the corner through the whole scene – is moving closer to the group.*

Agnes My story? You mean my chronicle? Well I'm famous for my otters. I have a mile of valley in the Cotswolds.

Simone Who's she talking about? / Who is ronicle?

Agnes Otters are incredibly versatile and intelligent. Otters are

Paula *is trying to speak, it seems.*

very very intelligent, very /ancient.

Hazel Ok, thank you . Did you travel for work Paula?

Paula No.

Hazel No? Ok?

Paula I'm a midwife. And I have five daughters. I am busy.

Hazel you/ were

Paula *now speaks to* **Agnes** *who replies to her.*

Paula My husband wouldn't leave me alone. So I have five daughters.

Agnes Yes, I have Asian short claw otters.

Simone Yeh well I worked every day of my life so your proverbs don't mean / shit to me.

Paula Too long ago.

Eugene Did someone mention Omar Sharif?

Hazel no / thank you no no

Fanta ah no.

Paula I

Eugene I thought, ah I thought that, we had . . . we were talking about Mexico? Mexico?

Agnes No, sir, we were talking about Kenya. About African civilisation . . .

Eugene Oh well.

Hazel have you travelled. Eugene?

Eugene .

I've been to Australia.

Hazel How was that?

Eugene Far away.

Short silence.

Paula I was an only child in the war.

Hazel Ok? That's good.

Paula But I was a girl guide.

After the war we did go on a camping trip in the south downs.

Beat, she thinks about it.

And that was pleasant

Agnes well?

Hazel So . . . there's been a few changes so I'm taking over the activities for now

Agnes YOU? what.

They are cutting everything

Simone lala la

Agnes they cut the entertainment the budget. We had more, before.

Paula Before.

Joan I see. Yes.

Paula *(tries to hit out)* RETREAT.

Hazel *(to* **Paula***)* shh it's ok.

But we have a lot of fun stuff planned /

Agnes *(to* **Joan***)* Last month, children from a school came to do a performance.

Shakespeare. You couldn't tell. But Simone / yes yes

Joan Oh, Shakespeare. Robert and I read him / together

Agnes ELOCUTION

Joan I beg your pardon / sorry

Agnes I had an excellent elocution teacher at school / if you want to sell anything / here

Paula My daughter Sharon does my banking.

Agnes And when I went to America / YOU HAVE TO SPEAK CLEARLY Everything here is cut back and there is nothing left to sell no

Aditi no / no no no no

Agnes Because we are in freefall.

Short beat.

Hazel We're doing an activity now.

Agnes well this is not good enough and I can't HEAR people. You have to use ELOCUTION . . . it's dragging . . .

Hazel *(aside to* **Fanta***)* make her put her hearing aid in next time.

Fanta I tried

Hazel *(to* **Agnes***)* we're doing an activity, I'm / trying

Agnes Excuse me. I beg your pardon. I sold my house to be here!

I'm going to go back to my room: I'm tired.

Eugene *follows* **Agnes** *out with little explanation.*

Joan Excuse me.

My family are coming to visit, and to pick me up . . . I'm just going to wait for them outside.

Fanta Hazel?

Joan Can you get my things from my room.

Open the door please.

Hazel *comes over to* **Joan** *and speaks to her gently.*

Hazel But, Joan, we told you, that you aren't allowed to go out of there . . . un-accompanied. You might get lost mightn't you?

Joan *freezes on the spot.*

Joan .

You never said that . . .

Hazel We did Joan, we told you last night, and this morning.

Beat, **Joan** *wonders if that is true, sudden panic.*

Joan You're a liar. Lynn! Lynn!

Simone They'll lock you up! I TELL YOU. lock you up. Let us out.

I won't jump under a train promise!

She makes her way over to the door, the rest of the residents are watching.

LET ME TELL YOU. They took me they put me. When I was SAD they put me in here / because I was cryin' torrential tears, torrents of bad.

Joan Who?

Simone The social. /

Hazel That is not true . . . Simone . . . you know that's not so simple

Joan I'm not here under any kind of duress you can't / just lock

Hazel It's / for your own good . . . it's safer

Joan NO! I will be allowed out

At this moment, a buzzer around **Fanta***'s neck (or in her pocket, similar) and a corresponding sound is heard off, from the corridor indicating that a resident is pressing an alarm to be given attention.*

Fanta ok sorry! Sorry.

Exit **Fanta**.

Paula BATHROOM! BATHROOM

Hazel Why don't you go to the garden, for a bit of fresh air?

Simone That isn't a garden

It's three sad sprouts in the shade. DYING dying. They put them /

Joan I WILL BE ALLOWED OUT.

Simone I told you they lock you up. I wanna see the light I'm not the pope but I want to be free. Not to Africa but let me go to the co-op

Abrupt change, shouts:

SIMONE SIMMONS

Hazel shh, Simone

Paula *is getting agitated.*

Paula I need to go!

Hazel Ok Paula!

Exit **Hazel** *with* **Paula**.

Simone It's true, But you'll see dey are nice. They sing songs to you even as they lock you up.

Goes to leave.

We'll be friends.

Joan *notices* **John**, *who hasn't moved through the entire scene and barely reacted to the tumult around him, as if he's been in his own world.* **John** *looks at* **Joan** *very intently and smiles. She is taken aback. But nods her head formally and politely.*

Blackout.

Scene Two

Two hours later. The same place.

Lynn *and* **Robbie** *are standing over* **Joan**, **Lynn** *and* **Robbie** *have clearly just arrived. Perhaps* **Lynn** *has her coat on, still. The image at lights up:* **Joan** *holding onto* **Robbie**'*s hand.* **Lynn** *a bit nervous and a bit off. She is holding a plant.* **John** *is sat in the corner still.*

There is music playing in the background.

Lynn *takes her coat off.* **Joan** *smiles at* **Robbie**. **Robbie** *looks around, curious.*

Joan I'm ready

Beat.

Lynn Shall we have a coffee or something here? Hello, Sir . . .

John .

Paula *wanders in and stares at the family.* **Lynn** *looks at her, smiles.*

Paula is it time for my pain killer?

Lynn I . . . I don't.

Paula No. No.

Exit **Paula**.

Another buzz on the door. **Fanta** *rushes back in – she was clearly in the middle of something –* **Laurie** *enters now and notices* **Fanta**, *then the care home. When he walks in, it's clear that his spirits drop, everything about the care home seems to upset him.*

Laurie Sorry yeah . . . I was having a smoke.

How are you, Grandma, good yeh this place is a bit of a fucking trip isn't it.

Lynn Shut up.

Robbie *has a packet of crisps in his pocket that he begins to eat.*

Beat.

Laurie it's ok if I like go check out the / place

Robbie we're here to see Grandma.

Lynn Sit / down

Laurie yeh but like maybe Grandma wants to go outside

Joan I can't move

Laurie Why can't you move?

Joan .

I've tried my hardest.

Laurie there's got to be some kind of doctor or psychologist that can fix you here / like you were before?

Joan no no.

Beat, then a movement as if **Joan** *is worried* **Lynn** *and the boys will leave.*

Joan Lynn I'm so happy you're here, it's magical to see you boys.

I'm happy to go . . . anytime you like we just need to get my stuff. I think on reflection, it's better I come home.

Beat. The family all look at each other. **Lynn** *seems to slightly panic.*

Lynn How is your room, Mum, there's a view, isn't there?

Joan of the car park, yes.

Lynn it's a big open space, you can see the sky!

Joan That's what they say in jail.

Laurie *laughs.*

Wanting to get the subject onto something more positive.

Lynn Robbie is going to football tonight, aren't you?

Robbie You said I could stop . . .

Lynn When? No I didn't. (*Laughs.*)

Robbie Dad said I could like stop / when

Laurie Yeah but like he's dead so who cares what he said.

Beat.

Enter **Simone**, *she stands there – does not sit down.*

Simone Fuck me there's a crowd.

Lynn Hi, I'm Lynn!

Simone Simone Simmons

They're gonna lock you up, Joanie.

Enter **Hazel**.

Hazel Hello there!

Lynn Hi /

Hazel Simone let's go up to your room / and let them have their visit

Simone I'm not doing anything. I'm sitting down.

Hazel Simone, please.

Paula *is upstage.*

Paula OLD! YEAR?

Hazel *wanders over to her. Shh.* **Simone** *is standing right in the middle of the room.*

Simone I'm in the corner and nobody is getting upset

Let me tell you I was fine this morning when I woke up. I was good. I was in a positive frame of mind. A positive frame of mind lady and then she goes and throws me under the fable.

The goddamn fable in the dark.

Joan The fable

Lynn The table?

Simone you deaf or something, love /

Lynn No, I'm so sorry

Joan Lynn, let's (go)

Simone can't you hear the dogs, there are packs of dogs barking in the night if you don't listen. Hell?

Hazel Don't . . . (pay attention to her) there aren't /

Simone Hey, Sweetie!

She is moving over to where **Robbie** *is.*

Robbie *starts up in fright.*

Simone He's a sweet little one . . .

Hazel Come on now /

Lynn Say hello, Robbie

Robbie Hello.

Simone I don't have no little 'uns. They all fell out (dead)

Suddenly emotional and full of complete commitment and truth:

Maybe you'll come and see me.

Robbie Why don't you / have kids?

Hazel OH . . .

Lynn don't ask that

Simone I haven't but I had lots a' lovers.

Hazel ok come on, I think that's enough.

She takes **Simone** *by the hand.* **Simone** *reacts to this a bit. She is led out, as if on autopilot.*

Hazel Don't mind her

Simone *wanders off, on* **Hazel***'s bidding.*

Hazel She's harmless /

Lynn ha, yes, (to **Joan**) she's / young

Hazel *exits. Beat.*

Laurie OK I'm off. This place is fucked

Robbie Why are you such a dick?

Laurie Jesus, can I at least check the place out?

Perhaps terrified of the idea of being left alone with her mother, **Lynn** *has a plant that she's carrying for the room.*

Lynn Hang on!

I've . . . got to go and put this in Grandma's room, you two boys / stay here and have a little chat / with her

Laurie What the actual fuck. / I mean

Lynn *is exiting.*

Robbie I need a pee pee

Lynn Come with me.

Laurie GREAT.

As an aside.

Lynn Stay here and talk to Grandmother, please. You need to spend a bit of time with her. Come on.

Joan Lynn! I need to speak to you.

Lynn *has already exited with* **Robbie**.

Lynn I'll be right back, Mum . . .

Laurie Mum!

Long silence. **Joan** *wets herself. Enter* **Fanta**, **Laurie** *catches her attention, flirts with her.*

Laurie Hey.

Fanta Hello.

Yes?

Laurie So, you like, working here / and like?

Joan Laurie . . .

Laurie Yeh.

Fanta yeh. So she's your grandma?

Laurie yeh. I mean . . . basically.

Fanta Basically?

Laurie Basically she's my grandma. Yeh.

Fanta ah! OK.

Have a great visit.

Beat. **Laurie** *wants to go and follow her.*

Laurie I'm just / going

Joan *gestures towards the bathroom.*

Joan Can you just . . . help me to the loo? They never seem to have time to take us . . . I can walk.

Laurie I think Mum is coming back soon

He goes over to her and tries to help her up out of her chair, but quickly gives up/is exasperated.

Laurie Fucksakes, Grandma, you're all messed up and like, Dad JUST died.

Joan Oh! Don't speak to me like / that!

Laurie Fuck Sorry

Joan The way you talk to people

Laurie Sorry

Beat.

Have you been playing your piano /

Laurie Can't be arsed.

Joan

that's a shame, your father loved your playing.

Laurie *rolls a cigarette.*

Beat.

Joan Isn't it today? (the anniversary)

Laurie This week, I dunno. Who cares.

Joan we care.

Laurie I mean, it's not like we're gonna DO anything

To mark it.

Joan Your mother said she was going to scatter his ashes.

You can't just leave him in a box / it

Laurie Why? Don't / talk about

Joan It's not good /

Laurie I know I know. Fuck.

It trails off, they know, this is a subject to avoid. **Joan** *seeks an ally.*

Lights flicker.

Laurie What the fuck?

Joan

This place is oh, it's awful, dear . . . I'm much looking forward to being home. I'm sure your mother is struggling, huh?

Laurie can't be *that* bad, like . . . how is the food?

Joan it IS dreadful.

Beat, and then feeling that this will give her a kind of credit.

what'll you have for dinner?

Laurie dunno –

Like to be honest probably pasta and ham and cheese.

Mum'll probably like get home and then like have a drink, and start talking shit and then we'll have an argument and then Robbie'll be like what is there to eat and Mum'll start a big panic and she'll say pasta because that's what she always says . . . and then we'll eat and there'll be a mess and at some point she'll cry and then she'll blame me for something, and then she'll throw the plate on the floor and then she'll go for a drive saying she's going to throw herself off a bridge, but she won't she'll just come back and drink more and then say how much she loves us and la la la and it'll be the usual shit, proper tragedy, you know.

Throughout this **Joan** *tries to interrupt and get him to stop speaking like this.*

Joan Stop stop!

Enter **Robbie**.

Laurie Alright, dick head

Robbie Hey, fuckwipe

Joan hello, Robbie, can you take me / to the bathroom . . . please . . . I just need help . . .

Laurie *pins* **Robbie** *to the chair and holds him down. The following is totally breathless and fast. It begins as play fighting but it develops*

Robbie you're so selfish oh my god, Laurie, I /

Laurie FUCK YOU /

Robbie I can't believe how selfish you are,

you were the same with Dad! /

Laurie Shut up, cunt

Robbie I hate you /

During this, **Robbie** *ad libs 'get off me, leave me alone!' etc.*

Laurie Look I was HERE talking to Grandma and you're not here and you just come in and think you know what's going on you have no idea what's going on at all. You're a fat cunt /

You're being a total fucking / shit

Total shit fuck you

Joan Do not TALK TO YOUR BROTHER LIKE THAT!!! DO NOT TALK TO YOUR BROTHER LIKE THAT

Robbie SHUT UP

Laurie He's a cunt, Grandma! It's his fault, ok!

They now fight, headlock, struggles but not actual punches. Or if there are punches thrown they are totally unsuccessful, they are half punches. Ad libs.

Robbie STOP IT! stop it ! Stop it!

Laurie ok ok you started it.

Fuck you

Robbie Grandma, would you like me to help you or I'll call a nurse.

Joan THANK YOU, DEAR. You are a good boy. I'll be ok.

Enter **Lynn**.

Laurie I'm just going

Lynn no you are not

Laurie I AM sorry but I am

Lynn no you are not you are staying here

Laurie fuc / ksakes.

Robbie You're such an arsehole.

Laurie *begins to shout 'AHH!!! Ahh!!' as if to silence the sound of the talking around him.*

Lynn mum

What is going on

Joan I told them to behave and to listen to each other but /

Robbie Laurie has been really so rude to Grandma, / he's been really nasty to her, really . . .

Joan Stop / shouting

Laurie *still shouting.*

Lynn ok ok

Mum just give me a minute

You need to calm down

Laurie I'm sorry but

You need to understand right (*Suddenly lyrical.*) I'm so tired of the . . . The . . . Dregs of the dead just lying around. SO tired of it. JESUS, Mum I'm sixteen. Sixteen YEARS old I don't want to have to deal with more death every year, Grandad, Dad, now her then what, you?

Beat.

Joan OH no well I will just die then, fine, I will just die then, that's ok.

You can get all your death over with and live forever.

Fool! Fool!

Robbie Shut up, Laurie, IT'S NOT ABOUT YOU

Laurie Mum, she's lost her fucking mind she has no idea what day it is.

Joan HOW DARE YOU! I'm absolutely fine / horrible boy

Lynn You can go / now

Laurie Where. Drive me to town

Mum fucking drive me to town

Lynn Go and calm down sit in the garden take Robbie and don't look in people's rooms.

Laurie .

Come on, fuckhead.

Robbie You're such a dick.

Laurie Come on.

They go out. Beat. **Lynn** *is exhausted. She might even be on the verge of tears.*

Joan You do your best.

Lynn *swallows. Gets her strength together then.*

Lynn It's ok here, Mum isn't it? I mean Hazel seems lovely, the activities and it's nice.

John *suddenly comes to life.*

John We never lost a match

Lynn Oh good

John Do you go to school with me?

Lynn No I – I didn't. I don't . . .

John We never lost a match at school. I thought you did, sorry.

Very sorry.

Enter **Robbie**, *eating a slice of chocolate cake. During the following* **John** *exits.*

Lynn My love, what's wrong? Why are you eating

Robbie nothing I'm fine

Lynn Where did you find that?

During the below, **Lynn** *looks over often to* **Joan**, *as if seeking affirmation.*

Robbie She said I could have it

Lynn Who?

Robbie I don't know, this old lady . . .

Lynn *panics that her child has stolen food from a patient. She takes the food off him.*

Robbie HEY! MUM!

Lynn Well you can't just take the . . . residents' food.

Robbie I didn't, Mum, she GAVE me the cake.

He slumps into a chair in the corner.

Lynn Are you ok, Robbie . . .

Was everything ok at school?

.

did Martin /

Robbie no they're my friends

He seems upset. There is a silence in which **Lynn** *looks towards* **Joan**, *as if to gather her strength.*

Lynn Are you missing Daddy, sweetheart?

No answer.

That's ok, today especially, to be upset, darling, really normal. Isn't it, Mum.

Robbie he died in his sleep didn't he . . .

Lynn yes

Robbie So maybe it was tomorrow, because it was in the night so it could be tomorrow. (The anniversary.)

Lynn yes, darling.

Robbie Are we going to do the ashes

Lynn Maybe not today, because . . . Grandma can't be there!

She looks towards **Joan** *for affirmation.* **Joan** *looks away.*

but soon we will, honey.

Robbie ok, Mum. /

Joan you can do it without me! You should go to that forest he liked!

Lynn I know . . . we will but not today I think . . . oh . . . haha!

She looks at **Robbie**.

Robbie *wanders off.* **Joan** *and* **Lynn** *are left alone.* **Lynn** *laughs a bit.*

Lynn That's a nice painting isn't it!

Joan No it isn't. ha!

Silence, they just sit there.

Joan This is a horribly furnished place . . .

Lynn Shall we have a cup of tea? / I'm going to have a cup of tea.

Lynn *goes and get herself a tea and biscuit from the side table. Perhaps as she does, a resident,* **Aditi**, *comes in (or is wheeled in) and sits in the corner muttering.*

Joan Cheap beyond belief.

The lady they put me next to at dinner last night was disgusting. And the / food

Lynn when Leon was spitting food everywhere you'd just leave the room.

Joan You shouldn't keep things from them.

Lynn *ignores this.*

Joan The woman had no class.

came to dinner in her pyjamas,

Lynn *laughs and immediately suppresses it.*

Lynn There ARE nice people here, I'm sure of it. You could get talking to them.

Joan NO no, I've never been good at making friends . . .

It was too late when you made me move.

Before **Lynn** *can say anything.*

Joan I'm perfectly capable of taking care of myself. Actually I could go back to my house . . .

Lynn Mum, you can't / it's sold

Joan I KNOW. Of course.

Eugene *walks through the space, looks at them fixedly, which makes* **Lynn** *feel like the space isn't so private.*

Lynn Do you want to go to your room?

Joan NO. It's dark in there. Darkness. You can't leave me here.

Beat, there is a change in the light and the shadows begin to move across the space.

They are very naughty you have to get a better handle on them you can't just let Laurie / run rings around you

Lynn I'm not, no-one is running rings around me. Oh I'm so tired

Joan you are doing your best, sorry. I know you need my help, when I'm back we'll sort them out.

Lynn I'm failing, Mum. I know.

I am a terrible mother.

I'm a terrible person . . .

Beat.

I don't like my / self

Joan no no / you just need to be tougher on them. If I could I would spank them blue.

They look at each other.

You've always needed help . . .

Beat.

I need to go back, I need to help you with the garden at least. It's a mess. Summer is coming and you told me you said we would do the garden together.

Dr Kenton said two weeks. /

Lynn She said six weeks and that's for a young person!

Joan I'll do the physio. It'll be fine . . . I've been doing the exercises

look

Joan *shows her some exercises.*

Joan I know you needed a breather. This is just respite care. I told them.

Lynn *nods but looks away.*

Lynn I've got to go back to work full time I can't just, they'll . . . let me go!

Things at work are good, I told you, I was there now that's why I'm late . . . you know my class is growing /

Joan I've spent some time here now and honestly this place is no good, /

Lynn I'm just talking. / about me

Joan I don't know why you help those people, your family needs you.

This place is going to slow my recovery.

Lynn No it isn't, Mum, it's not, you've been here one night! /

Joan *is taken aback, she confuses the time. But then, changing tone.*

Joan Darling come on . . . be reasonable. I've been here longer.

A look of panic comes over **Lynn**. *She looks around as if she is appealing for some help*

Lynn Mum, it's not just that . . . is it . . . it's not just your hip . . . I'm sorry.

Beat. Denial.

Joan We need to put the sweet peas in, now . . . You need to make sure you put a bamboo cane next to each one, so they grow up it!

I love the smell of sweet peas.

I love the smell of sweet peas.

Joan The top, the top terrace . . . the lavender, the sea pinks round the base of the sundial, the little veranda where you played and then the boys played . . . the most sun there . . . then . . .

The stone steps down, to the tomatoes

Lynn mum? What are you talking about?

Joan I'm talking about my garden in my house. My little rocky paths . . .

Ha! And the sea beyond it . . . down the road

Joan *thinks of the care home. Looks around.*

Lynn .

But, Mum, you've got a view of the garden here!

Joan I can't see it from the tiny little room they gave me. you got me the cheapest room I can't believe it / you didn't even

Lynn That's not true.

Joan The other place we went to visit was far better.

Lynn It's just this is a tiny bit more affordable for us / but I mean . . . it's all

(madly expensive)

She laughs nervously.

Joan Why didn't you get me a better room

Lynn I got you the best I could possibly get, I've cut RIGHT back, I'm doing my best, my best, Mum / fuck.

Joan I have money

Lynn .

Joan *gives* **Lynn** *a look as if to say 'don't you dare start'.*

Lynn I'm not saying anything.

Joan I have money, Lynn, I have money I do. I have the money from the house /

Lynn Yes and we're using that to pay /

Joan You mess everything up. Useless.

Lynn / Stop please

Joan I gave you my money

I want my money

My money

I want my money . . . I've given you everything

For Christ sake

What have you done with MY MONEY.

IT'S MY MONEY /

you can't put me in any old place. Even temporary.

Lynn what are we going to do

Joan I'll come home.

Lynn We've been over this, Mum.

Joan If I fall . . . the boys can pick me up?

Pause.

Lynn The neighbour had to call the ambulance because she heard you crying out. You have your button, your alarm why didn't you use it.

Joan the neighbour called.

Lynn it took twelve hours and you know that's not all . . . there is.

Joan I was just going to the toilet, if you and the boys had been home /

Lynn Mum! You kept falling. And I can't be there all the time, and . . .

I've just been with Leon, I just need a moment (without people in the house)

To you know to . . . live again really

Joan you went on your big trip.

Lynn yes that's what I'm saying; I came straight back after three days because you fell.

She looks away, as if she wants to leave. **Joan** *picks up on this.*

Joan .

It's just so magical when you're around, don't go.

Lynn I'll come and see you every day, Mum

I will

Joan oh no you won't. How can you do this to me. I'm perfectly fine.

Lynn mum!

Fucking hell

Fucking hell

Joan oh oh! Sorry Sorry ! there is so much shouting in your house! Stop! Why did I come. /

Lynn Mum stop just pushing me

Joan I'll be gone soon and you'll have to be alright without me darling. You'll have to be. My poor / Lynn oh dear

Lynn no no don't say that / !

Joan Lynn, I don't want to die here.

Lynn I'm sure you'll come back with us, Mum . . . soon. Just /

Joan I'd rather just die, if you don't want me there

Lynn *panics.*

Lynn mum please . . . no! I'm not ready for you to die

Joan well.

Lynn what would you like me to do?

Joan You said it –

Say I'll come home soon. Promise me.

Say so. I know what you're doing you're hiding me away! So you don't have to see!

Lynn .

Mum . . .

Joan SAY it.

Lynn Yes, of course, Mum. You just need to rest here, for a little bit, get a little bit better and we'll have you back . . . three weeks at most.

Joan Thank you. You'll talk to that woman when she comes in won't you, tell her (that it's a trial)

Lynn Where are the boys.

Joan They'll be along.

I don't want to die . . . not yet . . .

Joan Have you told Dad that I'm here, Robert will be worried. Tell him I'll call him this evening.

Lynn Mum, Dad is dead, he's been dead for years.

Joan I know.

I know, of course / that's not what I meant

Lynn Mum, Dad is dead.

Joan No . . . not . . . you're just saying that . . . Robert? You won't cheat me out of it /

Enter **Simone**, *almost hiding.*

Simone I'm telling ya I'm hunted.

She says this as she's going into the toilet. Clearly to hide. Enter **Hazel**, *chasing after* **Simone**, *looking for her.*

Hazel Oh hello, did you / see

Lynn she's gone out, I mean to the . . . (*She indicates the toilet.*)

Hazel *sees the look of panic on* **Joan**'*s face.*

Hazel ok ok

Shall we, maybe we should go to your room, eh? Help you settle in?

Hazel *takes over from* **Lynn** *here, it is a staggered process, involving, bit by bit taking the hands of the wheelchair away from her.*

Hazel Ok! You / need a hand

Lynn I can

Joan I want to go home!

She holds on to her daughter, won't let her go. **Lynn** *looks away.*

Lynn I'm sorry, Mum. Just . . . I'm here, Mum I'm here . . .

This calms **Joan** *who holds on to her daughter's hand.*

Joan My little daughter (you need me?)

She looks to **Hazel** *for some support,* **Fanta** *enters too now.*

Hazel It's ok it's ok

She looks at **Joan**, *right into her eyes.*

Hazel I know you're afraid . . . but you don't need to be afraid . . . I won't hurt you!

Joan three weeks, three weeks, but, I?

Lynn *is holding on to her mother's wheelchair.*

Hazel We've got this from here don't you worry yourself. Fanta, why don't you give me a hand . . .

Lynn OK. Yes. OK.

She lets go of the wheelchair. **Fanta** *takes it.*

Fanta here we are, Joan.

She takes **Joan** *out. Leaving* **Hazel** *and* **Lynn** *alone.*

Silence.

Hazel You alright there? Yeh?

Lynn *is a bit upset*

Lynn yes, no, yes, no sorry.

Hazel She'll be ok here/ you'll see

Lynn She just said my dad?

Hazel Sorry?

Lynn She thinks my dad is alive. Oh my god.

Hazel Oh, right, yeh, has it happened before?
At speed

Lynn There's been little things, she before she fell she'd wander out and we would get calls… what /

Hazel It's ok/ it's, it's

Lynn if she falls? What do I do? I can't have nurses /in the house.

Hazel it's common, one lady here does that . . . She's convinced her husband is still in hospital.. We don't tell her that he's passed./ Nah.

Lynn Yes, no, it's awful, It's hard. HA! Who would want to get old!

She laughs, the buzzer sounds in another room. Hazel is drawn to it

She.. is the room? If she needs to stay here i mean?

Hazel Yeah of course, we do have a room available for a permanent contract. One with the view?

The buzzer again

Lynn Yes, yes. Sorry do you need to

Hazel yeh but you can talk to the office about it? I'll ask/ them

Lynn Thank you, , thank you / thank you

Hazel Yeh no you're good, we'll sort it and you two can have a chat

Lynn Oh. Yes.

Hazel *is leaving, downstage this time. Then, after a time, out of the silence, the actress playing* **Aditi** *walks through the stage. She has a very neutral expression and walks in a light way. She is unseen by* **Lynn**, *to whom she remains invisible, and goes to sit in a chair in the audience where she will remain till the end of the show.*

Lynn *feels something in the air. She suddenly calls out for her children, perhaps there is a sound that is growing as she moves around looking.*

Lynn Boys! BOYS!

Come now! Come now! Boys!

WHERE ARE YOU? WHERE ARE YOU! LET'S GO

Lynn *looks out into the audience, looking for her boys in the people in the audience.*

Blackout.

Act Two

Scene One

The same place. The beginning of summer.

A group activity: movement and dance for the residents to encourage mobility. **Fanta** *is running the class and they are all doing choreographed, simple, movements to a song – the movements are linked to the song, almost miming the lyrics. For at least a couple of minutes, we just watch this.*

Joan *has a bag of things with her, clearly indicating her intention to leave.*

Fanta How you doing today, Mrs Taylor? You going to sing?

Joan I'm on the mend. I have my things /

Fanta yeh, I see that / are you going . . . (anywhere)

Hazel *takes over.*

Hazel YEH! She's come down now to be with her friend

Simone YEH, Joanie

Hazel You are a funny old couple aren't ya

Fanta *and* **Hazel** *aside (not heard by the rest of the room):*

Fanta She keeps saying she's going I don't know what to /

Hazel it's all good /

Simone *grins – we understand that a friendship is blossoming between them.*

Joan like music . . .

The class ends and **Hazel** *goes to turn the music off. General chatter.*

Hazel Well done, everyone

Agnes No I dare say that wasn't that bad.

Hazel And well done to Joan for coming down to join us! It's great to have you with us . . .

Joan Well, well . . .

If . . . if you can't beat them, join them . . .

Simone YEH!

Hazel That's lovely . . . and you're walking as well!

Joan I'm on the mend.

Hazel Well done.

Joan I'm going to show my family today . . . oh . . . I hope

Simone Coming are they, little 'uns? Ohh . . .

I'm off / home.

Paula *gets up and walks around lost. Then remembers that she has an idea, something she meant to say.*

Paula I rang the bell but you didn't no one was coming I was calling out, and I was sitting there in the piss, until eleven.

Fanta We're coming as fast as we can

Paula yes yes. And then when she came to wash me /

Fanta I came as quickly as I could

From here there are two simultaneous conversations.

Hazel How long are you spending /on getting each one down?

Paula I rang the / bell

Fanta 7-8 minutes

I have to change them - /when they've

Joan I find my bell hard /to reach

Hazel Yes but you can't /wash them FULLY -

Paula Fanta? Are you/

Fanta Just coming /Paula!

Agnes They don't put it back on the Table / . . . on the bedside table

Hazel Face hands underarm and pericare, that's it

Fanta Also I don't have enough wipes

Hazel One wipe per /person

Fanta No but. I'm going as fast / as I can

Agnes the bedside /table.

Hazel You remember what I told you

Fanta Six mins /per

Paula It's all so rushed

Fanta *(to PAULA)* We're doing our best. There's only two of us on shift today

Paula I know you're doing your best but -

Eugene I like running

Agnes Do you, sir?

Aside.

Fanta also, Agnes takes a long time to get dressed.

Light flickers.

Hazel they're meant to fix th / at

Agnes What did she say?

Simone She said sh' blew the doctor when he came to change her nappy as a fank you.

Agnes What?

Laughs. Including **Joan**.

Hazel Simone. Please.

Beat.

I need to talk to you all one minute just a moment please, I have something to tell you.

Paula What ?

Silence.

Simone Who's dead.

Beat.

Hazel Well, so /

Fanta yes / we

Hazel Thank you.

Do you know about Aditi?

Agnes No.

Fanta Mrs / Parekh.

Paula / No.

Short silence.

Joan What

Hazel She . . . passed on.

Fanta She's passed on.

Silence. Short

Agnes ah?

Simone Yeh so she kicked the bucket.

Hazel No but / Simone

Simone well

Hazel She's gone but we need to have some reverence, for her memory.

Simone I'm telling / the truth god knows I am

Paula Mrs Parekh?

Whispered.

Fanta She passed on.

Paula Oh. Right.

Hazel We, I, well what we could do now is write a card for her family.

Simone For the lamily?

Agnes It's true, there are people who go that we didn't even know

Hazel Would you like to write something on the card?

Agnes Yes.

Paula I will later.

Hazel Later.

Fanta Later.

Agnes I'm ninety-two and . . . yes, rather, sometimes I feel old.

Simone Yeh, love, you're next

Fanta Mrs Simmons, / Don't say that

Hazel SIMONE.

Simone how are you getting on with your luuuverboy, she's got his /

Fanta What?

Simone She's got his photo on her phone and she's got photos of him with his top off she showed me!!! At fancy places.

Joan I didn't know you / had a

Fanta shh! YOU'RE Embarrassing me . . .

Simone I told you Joanie. She's there, Lere, giggling, texting . . . SEXTING HIM! Fancy

Hazel well now we all know.

Very short pause. Solitude.

Fanta I'm really like so embarrassed oh my god / I'm not whatever you're saying him

Hazel yeh you're making a bit too much of it now aren't you. Don't know how you afford to go anywhere (on what we're paid)

Hazel *goes out for a moment.*

Simone Oh it's good isn't it SEX / AGHHHH!

Fanta you want me to put some music /

Agnes songs? Oh yes.

Joan is my family here? /

Fanta yes. not yet.

Who's got one they wanna hear?

No ?

Simone We going to do some singing now, that right?

Fanta yeh, what about . . .

I dunno, "Jingle Bells."

Simone Jingle balls. Jingle Balls hahahaha

Joan It's the middle of summer.

Fanta what about 'It's a Long Way to Tipperary'.

Paula no, I'm too old now. I don't know any songs

Fanta come on / Mrs Bailey you said you wanted a song.

Agnes I don't remember.

Fanta yes /

Hazel you liked to sing and dance didn't you, Joan? at home /

Joan I danced a few times, I did dance, I remember I danced, I did. Oh yeh, Que Sera Sera, Diana.

Pause.

Fanta Oh! You know it?

Joan I get these words sometimes they come to me, some of the songs.

Joan *speaks the lyrics to the chorus of 'Woodstock' by Joni Mitchell:*

Simone I LOVE JONI JOANIE HA she's my / soul

Fanta YEH? That's so cool

Joan yes, well I feel like the dog under the table and sometimes a scrap gets thrown to me.

Simone WOOFF

They laugh a little, suggesting their friendship has developed.

Hazel and you, John? Do you have an idea for a song / ?

Joan Hazel, is my family here now? I want to see them

Hazel I'm sorry

Your daughter / called she can't come. /

Joan why wasn't I told? Why not!!! Why not Why didn't you tell me.

I've been sitting here getting my hopes up, I got dressed up, you've let me sing and dance . . .

Hazel It's ok. I'm going to talk to her and get her to talk to you . . . yeh . . . it's all going to be ok.

Joan I feel like a fool. You knew and you didn't say anything. /

Simone don't be sad, Joanie.

Joan I wanted to see . . .

She looks at **Simone**, *almost takes fright.*

Joan I'M SICK OF YOU!

Simone .

No, don't say that.

She is hurt, she walks away. There is a silence. **Fanta** *helps* **Paula** *to leave.*

Hazel Come on now let's put some music on for John, yeh, why don't we do that. Would you like to listen to some music, John, or do you have an idea for a song we can sing?

John

I don't know . . .

Hazel But come on now, you LIKE music don't you?

You're in a bit of a slump today aren't you.

She caresses him, kisses him on the head like a baby.

John. Oh

A small smile, a very tender moment.

Hazel Mrs Francis

John *says nothing, but a tiny change of rhythm takes place in him, he moves a little . . . very little, but enough to say that it is a reaction.*

but yes

Ah, I remember

Maybe . . .

She puts on 'Some Enchanted Evening' for a moment, we all listen to the introduction, calmly.

Agnes Oh

Hazel You know this one don't you, Agnes ?

Agnes Yes

Hazel You know it, don't you ?

No reaction. Then **John** *starts singing slowly. Then loudly and with emotion. It is a real solo. It is very moving, as if he has come to life from the music. At a moment in the song he looks over to* **Joan**.

Hazel wow!!!

oh it's wonderful

Fanta *enters from the corridor, it's funny, she enters in the middle of the song.*

Fanta Mr Francis!!! Oh my god what!!! I didn't know! wow !!!!

Hazel You like your music /

Fanta he sings so well doesn't he.

Agnes Yes

Simone no we didn't think he / could

Agnes It didn't occur to me that he would sing.

John *stops singing. He doesn't reach the end of the song.*

Hazel You a singer?

John No, I don't know, no no.

Fanta When did you learn to sing?

John I don't know

Hazel yeh you do . . .

John *looks at the two, starts to cry.*

John I'm no-one

I'm nothing I'm lost.

Pause, he cries.

Astonished.

I'm crying.

Smiling.

Fanta Don't cry, Mr Francis

Hazel Why are you crying?

John. Oh, I don't know.

I love

EVERYONE. Here.

Moved.

That's my gang

That's my gang

Simone oh he's crying /

Fanta yes

Simone He's crying? Then he's living.

John No no

I'm not crying

I'm TOUCHED.

Joan I was very touched too. You brought joy to us . . .

I feel joy.

Beat. **John** *looks at* **Joan** *and smiles.*

Simone I'm touched too. YEH!!!

I NEVER saw you like that, that way.

You're handsome, you're like a little bit of sunlight on a stream . . . Why am I fad. Lick your neighbour as thyself!

Joan No but I / want to say

Hazel aw yeh, that was really touching. /

Fanta yeh that was touching.

Hazel yeh really like touching oh my god.

Really was . . . / yeh

Fanta yeh

Fanta *exits,* **Hazel** *follows, so that for a moment* **Joan**, **Simone** *and* **John** *are left alone.*

John. I like music

In the following there is a kind of competition between **Joan** *and* **Simone**.

Joan I . . . / wanted to

Simone Yeh I LOVE music, you know in the summertime, by the liver, in the mommertime humpy bumpy getting all close and TOUCHING fucky

Singing in the manner of a nursery rhyme, making a point of stressing the rhyme and repeating with glee

Lickety fucky/fuckety dicky doo . . . arsehole, cunt and tongue too.

Joan Simone I'm / trying to talk please please PLEASE

Simone I LOVE dancing, you know up close and personal and all when you can feel All the other person oh yeh

She has got up and she's dancing. **Hazel** *re-enters.*

Simone / And you're on the river and it's dark

Hazel NO But /

Joan I also wish / to speak I want to say things too, I have things I wish to say

Hazel Alright / LADIES

Simone I like all them musics the whole thing Rock and Roll, Dance Music music music and sound too

She's lost for a minute, then, as if she's just remembered a crucial fact about herself that she thought she had forgotten.

I LOVE COUNTRY MUSIC. I LOVE COUNTRY MUSIC.

John What? / What are you saying be quiet please please please

Simone la la la la I mean

She begins to sing

Hazel You're not alone in here

Joan I want to talk . . . / I have something to say!!! I do!

Simone I've been all sorts of places! I have / lalala

Hazel *comes over, it's getting a bit tense.*

Joan EVERYONE interrupts, I'm pushed to the side and I feel like I'm – I'm hunting for scraps / under the table

Simone I woudda lived in a shoebox if someone had loved me right. la la la 'Come and suck my dicky dicky! lala my dicky LALALALA'

Agnes stop your, your lalala

Singing, and this can repeat, change melody, it can go on for a beat or two, **Agnes** *ad libbing 'stop',* **Hazel** *saying 'there there' or similar.*

Simone We're all gonna die die die die! We're all gonna die!

LALALA

we're gonna die! We're all I say, we're all gonna die! Lala die die dye dye lalla we're all gonna die

Joan STOP!

Simone go fuck yourself.

She is suddenly upset like a little girl.

Hazel ok, ladies. SIMONE come with me now, come on.

Come with me!

Simone Stabbing stabbing blood and fuck.

Let's go out into the garden.

Exit **Simone** *and* **Hazel**.

After the chaos, **Joan** *and* **John** *are left alone.* **Agnes** *exits slowly during this.*

Joan I . . . upset her . . . oh no.

I was just getting my bearings and I wasn't expecting to find your voice so beautiful. But your voice! Oh your voice! (*Beat.*)

John Forgive me. My darling.

Joan .

I have meant to come and sit near to you but well the occasion hasn't presented itself.

John No, indeed.

I do wish you had.

Short silence. She's not sure why he's looking at her so intently.

John Oh . . .

you know

Joan I am not someone to argue and be bitter. Oh . . . I hope.

Beat.

Joan *looks over at the door, then back to* **John** *who is smiling at her.*

Well you're looking at me rather strangely now

John *laughs, so does* **Joan**.

Joan I /

John I thought you were so nice then, before though, in your blue dress

Joan I'm sorry.

John I'm crying, I'm crying, you were in your blue dress

Where was it . . .

Nice!

Joan *becomes aware that something is being made up but goes along with it.*

NICE!!!

It was Nice

We were staying down the coast at Menton, we crossed back on the little rickety train that goes by the sea . . .

we walked up the ramparts

Joan Sorry?

John And I asked you if you wanted to go on, and we had no idea where we were going

He begins to weep.

And the next day, we had lunch on the balcony of your hotel room, it was the nicest lunch I have eaten in my life, my love.

Joan what did we eat?

John tomatoes

But there was the sea.

John *is silent, they are sitting there, as if they can imagine the sea now. Maybe* **John** *takes her hand.*

They are suspended, in a loving gaze towards one another, it feels like anything could happen but, just then, there is the violent buzz of the doorbell.

Fanta *enters and lets them in. Enter* **Lynn**, **Robbie**, **Laurie**. *They have a big white plastic bag with them . . .*

Fanta Hello Mrs Sadetski!

Lynn Sorry we're so late Laurie / was

Fanta I thought you said you couldn't make it

Lynn Yes! Mum!

Lynn *hugs* **Joan**, **John** *is weirdly very close, holding* **Joan**'*s hand.*

Robbie Grandma

Laurie Hey

Lynn *(to John)* Hello

Enter **Hazel**, *who has heard the doorbell.*

Hazel we actually got your mum down again . . .

Aside.

Did you speak to / her ?

Before **Lynn** *has a chance to answer* **Joan** *speaks.*

Joan I've been down many times. But last time you didn't come and they said you cancelled this time. I'm on the mend. I want to / show you

Lynn I'M SO sorry, we're here, Mum, aren't we?

John *is still holding hands with* **Joan**.

Joan I'm on the mend. So . . . (I'm ready)

Fanta Do you want to come with me for a walk, Mr Francis, come on come on . . .

Hazel *looks over at* **Lynn**, *to suggest that she should speak to her mother.*

Lynn *looks away.*

John .

Fanta *leads* **John** *off.*

Joan *clings to* **Hazel** *and does not let her go.*

Hazel Here /

Joan Yes, hold me

Hazel Come on, you're ok. OK, ok here you are

Lynn Mum? We're here, Mum?

Hazel *untangles her.*

Joan I'm sorry I don't want to be here. / I'm

Hazel Joan! your family is here! Look the kiddies are here /

Laurie I'm not a / kiddy

Hazel see they're all here! Come on . . .

Lynn Mum /

Hazel I've gotta get going now / I've got

Robbie I'm gonna play the cello for you and stuff, Grandma. I said I would / you know

Hazel oh that'd be nice wouldn't it you know we're always looking / for people to do some entertaining here!

Laurie yeah Robbie's gonna play, he's gonna play /

Paula *wanders in at some point below,*

Lynn thank you

She goes over to her mother and begins stroking her.

Lynn You're alright aren't you, Mum,

Joan Are we going to walk in the hills.

Lynn Yes, Mum.

Robbie I'll like play the cello /

Laurie Yeh I could even like play something maybe like there is a piano and stuff /

Lynn WOW, god well that's really something now if you've got Laurie saying that. I mean wow.

Joan oh I'd like that.

Lynn Yes, Daddy loved it when you played /

Joan It's magical watching you grow up . . . Laurie has changed . . .

Lynn We were just here / he's handsome!

Laurie Like two weeks ago, Grandma. Shut up.

Joan No, it was a month ago.

Then, suddenly, afraid.

You've abandoned me! They are abandoning me!

Hazel No they're not! OK, I'll let you all have a little chat.

She exits, with another look at **Lynn**.

Beat.

Laurie let's give her the / thing

He rushes to do it.

Robbie I want to give it to Grandma. (*The children grapple over the bag which* **Robbie** *was carrying.*)

Lynn Give it / Laurie stay back

Joan Be sweet to your brother / be sweet.

Laurie He can fucking do it! I didn't say nothing.

Robbie *goes to the white plastic bag containing the TV and takes it out.*

Robbie Tada!

They're bringing out the TV, it's beige/yellow.

Lynn Look LOOK, Mum! It's yellow! like the walls of your room . . .

Laurie *makes fun.*

Laurie LOOK . . . grandma. It's yellow! Oh! Oh! It's yellow like the walls of your room.

Joan I didn't paint that room it's not my room.

What make is it . . . a Sony?

Lynn *(lying)* Oh I dunno.

Robbie I'll plug it in

Lynn Not here, Robbie / Let's wait until

Robbie *looks for a plug in the room.*

Laurie Fucksakes, Mum.

Robbie / There's no plug.

Joan Hold on . . . Why do I need a TV, / I have one at home.

Lynn hold on, not in here, we'll do it in her roo / m

Laurie Look (*He has found a plug socket.*)

You little fuck

Robbie WAIT I'M ALMOST DONE

Joan I've always had a Sony, I don't know what you're doing to me . . .

Robbie *and* **Laurie** *are under the table now.*

Robbie *bangs his head.*

Robbie Ow

Joan I've always had a Sony

I don't . . . what are you . . .

Lynn Mum it's yellow hang on, though it's yellow I thought that cos the / walls

Laurie What's up, Grandma?

Joan No no you took all my money and you're spending it all, throwing me a bone like a dog under the table you're throwing me a bone with a cheap old TV! Bloody Bloody I won't have it no sir I won't have it, you just want to bury me here! You want to bury me here, and you're not even giving me a Sony, you're just burying me with your fakery and with this cheap lie . . . TV! You think you can hide me away here! And not face REALITY! REALITY

No no no no no / no no no no

Lynn Mum Mum

Laurie Calm down!

Grandma! Grandma! Calm the fuck down. Mum, Jesus, you haven't even spoken to her

Lynn *laughs nervously.*

Laurie Tell her the fucking truth. Tell her, Mum, Grandma you need the TV

Joan I have a perfectly TV tv at home.

Laurie You can't come home, Grandma.

Robbie I GOT IT TO WORK I GOT IT TO WORK

The TV turns on something quite funny: maybe a wildlife documentary about a flock of birds. During the next beat **Robbie** *fiddles with the remote and changes the volume on it.*

Lynn Turn it off / turn it off

Joan It's not a Sony, it's what IS /

Lynn It's a (*Lying.*)

A . . . I don't know a

Pro Lite . . . LCD monitor

Joan that I've never heard of and / I have a TV.

Lynn Mum you don't have a TV / and I need to, please calm down.

Joan It's not about the TV it's about how I FEEL! You tricked me.

Lynn Mum! I've tried to talk to you many times. I've told you, it's hard for you to be with us.

Joan You're useless. Useless.

Joan *is upset, so she pushes the TV on the floor. It breaks.*

Lynn Why did you do that?

Joan I didn't want to.

Robbie Ow

Lynn are you hurt?

Robbie .

Almost.

Lynn Mum, what d'you do that for.

Joan I don't know . . . I didn't want to push it over

Quiet, the kids are picking up the TV.

Laurie like it maybe still works

Joan I don't want it. You think you can just pay me off with cheap stuff and lock me away, you lied to me.

Lynn Mum! I can't!

you can just stare at the walls.

Beat.

Joan I'm not dead!

Lynn Mum, please . . . please . . .

Joan What?

She looks around her and realises that she's not leaving.

You think you can decide how my life ends.

Well, you can't. I'm not having it / it's not righteous.

Lynn What?

Joan Nothing is righteous: you just think you can lie to people

I bet you still didn't tell them how their father died, did you? you're lying to everyone!

Lynn Mum?

Joan You still didn't even tell them about Leon

Laurie What about Dad?

Lynn Nothing

Joan see you didn't

I always thought it would be challenging for you to have children. you aren't very strong / . . . You have to grow up one day.

Lynn I am!

Joan No I'm just saying /

Laurie What.

Lynn .

Laurie What the fuck, Mum.

Lynn I won't there's what –

I

Laughs loudly.

Sorry.

I don't know what to do or say / I just

Laurie What you laughing at /

Lynn I, well, I was just saying.

(Then realising now that there's no way out of telling them.) Honey.

Laurie .

He is suddenly very quiet.

Lynn darling? Laurie . . .

Laurie .

Lynn I wanted to tell you something, darling

Joan LYNN

Lynn I

Well, the day Daddy died I was

Robbie Mum, don't

Lynn I was very, very tired.

(Almost convincing herself.) I was, baby

I'd always stay with him when he was in the shower. I'd walk him in, sit him down on the seat, and the water'd start and he'd smile at me and take the shower head but that time he wanted me to wait outside.

I sat on the bed and I was so tired.

Laurie .

Lynn And I closed my eyes – I wasn't going to fall asleep no

Laurie What / you

Lynn He didn't want people there he didn't he wouldn't have people there . . . he was frightened of the respite carers. But they told me I had to be there to keep an eye. But I . . .

Laurie What did you do to him!

Lynn When I came back he'd collapsed.

I was shocked I'd fallen asleep. I am so ashamed darling. So ashamed. Please . . .

Robbie .

I knew he didn't die, like, in his sleep.

Laurie She told you

Robbie no I just worked it out.

Lynn REALLY? baby

Laurie you were probably drunk for fuck sakes

Joan Don't say that about your mother / but at

Lynn I /

Joan well at least now you told them, I always said that you should tell them. You can't blame yourself but you can't give them a version of things / the truth has to be out it's better for all of you

Lynn *rushes over to her mother and shakes her violently.*

Lynn MUM !!!

MUM MUM MUM!!!

Beat.

Sorry, Mum

Laurie *runs out of the room.*

Lynn LAURIE!

Robbie What the fuck

Hazel *enters.*

Hazel why is there a TV /

Lynn We're leaving. Mum, I got you a room with a view.

Exit **Lynn**, **Robbie** *follows.*

Joan My baby!

Hazel It's all right, it's all right

Hazel *tries to comfort her.* **Joan** *sits down.*

The lights flicker, **Hazel** *looks at it.*

John *enters*

Hazel Yeh you sit yourself there. Don't be upset. She's doing her best . . . you need the help we give you here.

Joan She will never come back to visit me now.

Hazel They will! You'll see. Oh, Joan.

John You are so beautiful so beautiful

Hazel John this isn't the best time yeh.

Exit **Hazel**.

John You are a goddess

Joan I . . .

I do not know what to do

You are being so kind to me.

John We're so happy.

We're so happy.

He undresses.

Joan what are you doing?

John I want you to see me I have no

Shame

No shame at all

He is undressed, standing in front of her arms outstretched.

I just want to hold you in my arms

Gently, slowly, he walks to her. He has trouble walking. Slowly he holds her, they hold each other. It is very gentle.

Jennifer! MY JENNIFER

Joan My name isn't Jennifer, you know that?

John .

Beat. He goes as if to move away.

Joan But that's ok

I like you holding me

She holds on to him, like she won't let go of him.

Maybe you can just hold me . . . please please

John *holds her but then is upset, feeling lost . . . like he has come out of it.*

John Sorry

I don't know what to say about this . . . I feel so much . . .

Joan No, I . . .

She looks at him as if to say don't go.

John is this just a hole.

A hole in the heart into which you fall and you go on falling.

Joan you're gentle.

They embrace for a time, it is quite silent during this.

John. I'm crying.

I don't know why I'm crying. But I feel I'm crying.

Whispered.

My heart is so full /

I feel love.

Joan There is love.

Even for a minute.

Enter **Hazel**.

Hazel Oh, John! Come on, let's get you dressed

John OH!

Fanta oh my god! Oh my god!

Fanta *laughs.*

Hazel SHH. Get him out

Fanta Let's go and listen to some music

John Oh . . .

Hazel He thinks you're his wife, Joan you know that don't you . . . for god sakes.

Pause.

John I don't know, I don't know anything about that – I don't know anything about that.

Hazel Come on now, let's get you out of here

Fanta We're going to listen to some music let's go listen to something

John No no . . . oh? Love? Somewhere?

Fanta come on let's go to the music

Hazel *and* **Joan** *are left.*

Hazel Joan.

You know that . . . that isn't ok. You shouldn't go along with that kind of thing.

Joan I don't know what happened.

Beat, ashamed but touched.

He just held me, he just held Me. He knew it was me. He saw me.

The broken TV is on the ground.

What is the way home Hazel?

Blackout.

Scene Two

The same place.

Late September.

Lunchtime.

The common room.

People who can't eat by themselves wait to be fed, but they have to wait a long time.

Fanta *feeds* **Paula**. *Total silence for a long while.* **Joan** *is not there.*

A long silence.

Eugene, *in this section, is standing at the table where* **Agnes** *is sat. He eats and then sort of wanders around.*

Fanta Open up

Mrs Farr come on now open up.

Hazel *enters.*

Hazel the temps still haven't shown up

Fanta oh sorry! I spilt that, sorry there

Hazel (*to Agnes*) You want me to rub your hand?

Agnes yes . . .

Hazel You said your husband rubbed your hand like that.

Agnes Is he out of the hospital?

Simone HAZEL can I mave lanother napkin . . .

Hazel *brings the napkin over.*

Hazel *(about* **Paula***)* Did she eat or didn't she.

Fanta I mean she's sort of eating . . . I guess.

Paula *spits out her food.*

Hazel *(aside)* It's the UTIs they just floor them, she got worse quick bless her

Simone Gimme another wine sweetheart . . . go on. Where is Joanie

Hazel *goes to get the wine.*

Hazel Alright then but then we're done here ok, Simone

Simone What's 'is name.

Eugene EUGENE

Simone Gene's havin another too

Eugene I loooove lentils with sausage.

Hazel *has brought the wine. Pours it for both of them.*

Simone Where's JOAN

She not coming out of her room

John *begins to cry like a baby.*

Fanta You ok, Mr Francis?

John My mother said not to volunteer or anything . . .

Fanta Oh no . . .

Simone What's on tele later?

Eugene I don't know.

Simone ah What's om Tuesday

"Countdown" innit. Nah it's

"A House in the Sun."

The light flickers.

(Confused.) Where's the bathroom?

(Perhaps tries to undress.)

Hazel SIMONE.

Simone Don't fuck with me, HAZEL

Hazel There.

Fanta Come on John

Simone *goes to the toilet. Silence.*

Agnes Forgive me.

No response from anyone.

Eugene oh yes, oh yes,

Short silence. Eugene moves in one direction then as if he's had a thought, in another.

Agnes Otters are very versatile creatures. There are thirteen kinds of otter . . .

Enter **Joan**. *She is now a diminished figure.*

Eugene Ah. I like.

John I liked it when she'd wear nice skirts

Fanta ah yeh?

John my secretary . . .

We hear the sound of rain falling.

Fanta Oh my god.

Silence, They look up.

Hazel Yeh. It reminds me, actually, yeh, like this one time, I went on holiday with my son, yeh it rained every day

Agnes Rainy Season

Simone *comes back out of the toilet.*

Long pause, they all look up at the roof, where we imagine that there is rain.

Simone *is kind to* **Joan**.

Simone Joanie do you want to sit with me, yeh? yeh?

Joan yes . . .

She looks around here, she's a bit confused.

I'm lost.

Simone She needs a drink . . . did they call.

John Cold.

Simone *is reaching over, or walking over to* **Eugene***'s area and taking his glass of wine.*

Hazel Simone . . .

Simone WHAT . . .

Hazel No you can't have another

Simone Ah it's because My mam / Well my mam was into her thirst, she liked a drink so.

Hazel /no it's not

Simone Well my mam was into her thirst, she liked a drink so.

Joan ah / her mum you see

Simone it's true sometimes I have a need, / sometimes I get thirsty

Hazel / don't you just

Joan Yes

Looking over at **Hazel**.

Simone She's nice to me sometimes but then she knocks me. Slamming the door and it frakes my heart.

Like a little girl.

My little Kart.

John Cold. Cold. Colder. Cold . . .

Fanta OK come on everyone let's have a sing song.

Hazel Yes . . .

Simone Music

Hazel Yeh it's miserable outside isn't it. Summer is really over now.

Fanta September is always like "School lol". Rain.

Agnes Hazel.

Agnes *looks around, lost. She touches her face, as if to ensure that she is 'in order'.*

My hair . . .

Hazel *goes to her and brushes her hair.* **Agnes** *is happy.*

Suddenly the lights go off. In the set design, it should be clear that this is caused by the fault pointed out earlier, and the intermittent flickers, as part of the general state of disrepair. Dialogue that follows piles in on top of itself. Ad libbing is helpful too.

Fanta *turns on her phone, it's the only light we can see in the audience.*

Fanta it's all good, all alright . . .

John *just makes his way out of the room.*

Simone WHAT HAPPENED WHAT HAPPENED

Hazel the lights . . .

Fanta oh!

We see **Fanta***'s light getting agitated around* **Paula***, who is completely still.*

The light comes on suddenly, from another source.

Simone WHAT'S she gowt now?

Simone *turns around, looking away, not wanting to see. But* **Joan** *is drawn towards* **Paula**.

John oh! Oh!

Hazel Give us some room move yourselves

I'm going to go and get a doctor I'll go and get /

Exit **Hazel**.

Fanta don't rush everybody that's what Hazel's gone to do! She's doing that and Mrs Farr has just had a shock

Eugene *leaves, following* **Hazel**.

Joan *is stuck, staring at* **Paula**.

Fanta I swear it's ok, I'm sure

Aren't you

The actress playing **Paula** *stands up and walks gracefully to sit in the audience, as* **Aditi** *did before, where she too will remain till the end of the show. The others continue to believe her body is still on the chair.*

Fanta *takes the pulse of the now imagined body on the chair, realizes she's dead, looks up at* **Joan**. *Everyone else has gone but* **Joan**. *Who is somehow witnessing the dead.*

Fanta Mrs Taylor you shouldn't be here don't look . . .

Joan .

I can't look away.

Blackout.

Scene Three

The same place.

Some hours later. **Joan** *and* **Simone** *stand facing out staring into the distance.*

Simone Something ain't right

Joan No / no it isn't

Simone NAH

Then speaking together.

Simone/Joan Nah/no

Simone Can you hear the dogs? Them dogs barking?

Joan *is in another part of the stage.*

Joan wait?

They listen, there is nothing.

Simone Do you hear them?

They listen.

Joan I heard them. Last night.

I woke up . . .

Simone did ya?

Joan Yes . . . oh . . .

I called all night . . .

Joan I called /

Simone You called?

Joan I called! I did.

Simone You called?

Joan I called! I did. I don't sleep.

Joan *tries to walk, she has a stick but she is tottering, stumbling a bit. Struggling, overall. She sways.*

Oh!

Simone don't go.

Simone *goes over to* **Joan**, *tries to help her; it should feel a bit like the blind leading the blind.* **Joan** *is unsteady. Beat.*

Joan I am on the mend.

Simone don't go /.

Joan no.

Pause.

Simone There's a leak in my head, Joan. My head is dripping.

Do you want your biscuit.

Joan *doesn't answer. She takes the biscuit that* **Simone** *is handing her. After a short time, enter* **Hazel** *with a wheelchair for Joan.*

Joan I PRESSED THE BUTTON FIFTEEN MINUTES AGO! /

Hazel I'm sorry . . .

Do you want to sit? Joan, do you want to sit down?

She tries to get **Joan** *into a wheelchair.*

Joan I don't want to sit in that, it's for cripples!

Simone I have always felt close to dogs and children.

Men don't cut it.

Hazel Go to bed, Simone. (*She yawns.*) I want to go to bed

I been here a day love. Double shift. Twenty hours.

Beat.

Simone The first time I thought I was dead, I was in Swansea.

Joan His name was Paul, my first husband

Paul

Simone Paul /

Joan he was in the Navy and we were married seven years, Lynn doesn't know / about it

Simone OH / no, yeh . . . I won't tell her.

Joan he was always the last off the ship, and we went for a walk and we were walking on the cliff and he tried to push me off it /

Hazel Oh wow . . .

Joan I mean I felt it, I felt he was trying to do that I didn't . . .

Beat.

Hazel But an / d you remarried

Joan I met my second husband and he wouldn't hurt a fly. He was a gentle one. Robert. He was a tall glass of clean water . . . just when you're thirsty . . . Lynn loved her daddy. At least.

Hazel It's good that you have some good memories to call on!

Joan I have had some good / times

Hazel Some good times, yeh! yeh.

Shall I put a bit of music on.

Simone I could've been killed too! it's / not just her

Joan In those days I'm telling you /

Simone But I know what fo protect / myself, little 'un, you know

Hazel Simone / like

Simone Turn a situation around before it gets outta control / never let your eye down

Joan No / in those days . . . you let things

Simone There are a lot of men who think about killing a woman . . . they get hot and they need to lash out at a woman /

Joan oh yes

Simone but that was what I was there for.

Short beat.

Hazel Come on, Simone . . .

Simone If you don't have love you always have people to hit you. no no

Joan Why is there so much pain in life /. Life

Simone My / life and my blood is full of life.

Joan I shouldn't have left my house. My home. Everything was safe, 'Robert the gentle'.

Pause, silence. There is still a bit of rain. **Hazel** *has a phone out and is handing it to* **Joan**.

Hazel ok. Come on now.

Joan *rejects the phone being handed to her by* **Hazel**

Why don't you call your daughter?

Come on, what about writing a letter, an email, I'll help you?

Joan No.

No reaction from **Joan**

Hazel It's been what three months?

Simone nearly four. Fall for.

Hazel Yeh.. that's a long time.

Beat

Joan I never find the words.

Simone *gets a pen off* **Hazel**, *who sort of giggles.*

Dear Child, oh, dear Child, please come to table, dinner is ready, and . . . and your mummy is waiting for you, to eat. To draw.

because / i am hungry

Joan Stop.

Simone No i'm helping! "I WANT you to come and see me. And my friend Simone Simmons. Bring a bottle and a grin/ to have a gin

Joan Stop it!

Joan *snatches the piece of paper off* **Simone**.

Hazel She's being nice..

Simone no no Joanie no don't. Not again/ not again not again

Joan I want to go to my room.

Short silence.

I'm going.

I'll go. I'll go.

Holding the letter.

It's too late.

Simone Please no no Joanie, please please. Stay with me, we can run away.

Simone *hangs on to her.*

Joan No.

Simone Say you love me say you love / me say you do.. Joanie!

Joan I'm going to fall

Hazel Shh.

Hazel *separates them.* **Joan** *is leaving*

Simone But love! mummy and dark of the bite! The dog bite.

YOU SAID YOU HEARD THEM!

Hazel Shh, it's ok darling , co/me on now let go of her she'll be back

Joan Get off me.

Simone *does, resignedly.*

I want to go to my room

Simone *makes to go after her.*

Simone Please (mummy)

Joan .

Exit **Joan** *with* **Hazel**. **Simone** *is left for a moment alone on stage, and now seems to be almost in a dialogue with herself at quite great speed.*

Simone FRIEND? TO? Or?

But you have friends.

No you don't/

You just go to darkness!

Help?

Hazel *re-enters.*

Hazel she's just upset.. Doesn't mean anything.

Why don't you go to your room, Yeh? No get some rest/

Simone NO not my room.

Simone *looks around to check no-one can see.*

Simone someone cut into my heart and is bleeding me dry.

Hazel No no

Simone If I was in charge, I'd run us all away from here

Someone has to be to blame for what's happening to us. I want someone to be responsible . . . so I can ask them for mercy. I tried a lot of things.

Do you hear the time talking.

Hazel Do you want me to turn on the TV? Do you? (*Stroking her.*) We could have you watch a bit of telly yeh . . .

Simone NO

Hazel I know let's put your favourite music on.

Simone You're MY FAVOURITE HAZEL!

Simone *takes off her earrings, and her bracelet, her jewellery, maybe a necklace too.*

Hazel Oh those are nice.

Simone You take these here things, they're from Simone Simmons, my little heart, I ain't got no-one else / to give 'em to . . . you take 'em

Hazel Oh Simone, I can't

Simone No no, I want you to have them. You're everyone and you're pretty, you will get a Loverboy too a Loverboy, fucky fucky.

Hazel OH! Stop it . . .

Beat.

Simone you'll wear them, so they won't disappear

Hazel I can't take them, darling –

Simone No, no. It's time talking it's walking in me.

Hazel *takes them firmly in her hand. Starts putting them on as a sign of respect to* **Simone**.

Simone Oh.

it's a gift from the lenter of my heart. The centre of my dart.

In the dark.

Hazel .

thank you

Hazel *exits, continues with her work.* **Simone** *is alone. After some trepidation, She breaks the fourth wall, and unlike the others, we understand that she is the one choosing to go into the audience, into the other world. She looks at us as she walks through the audience and sits half way up the seating bank. As she passes audience members, she stares at some of them, as if asking them what is happening to her or seeing people from another life, as she goes into the other world, where we all go.*

Blackout.

Act Three

Scene One

The scene has shifted to **Joan***'s bedroom in the home.*

December.

The light turns on and reveals **Joan** *on the floor.*

Lynn *and* **Robbie** *are standing over her.*

Joan Lynn? / Lynn?

Lynn I'm here

Joan Where is Lynn?

Hazel Watch yourself

Lynn WHAT HAPPENED

Robbie Mum!

Joan Why didn't you come / every day

Lynn I'm here, aren't I? I . . . Have come to see you

Robbie I'll come to see you all the time, Grandma. I really want to come and see you /

Lynn Mum, what did you do?

But I come see you!

Looks at **Hazel**.

Lynn I come see her!

Hazel I'm not saying anything, Mrs Sadetski. I'll let you talk to your mother. But if people don't come see them . . .

She exits, a little upset.

Robbie We came, Grandma, we are here me and Mum

Joan Yes, dear, no.

Lynn Mum, what have you done?

Robbie Grandma, can I move her, can I move you up a little, even a little bit?

Lynn no, no, we shouldn't

Mum, Mum

What did you do?

Joan *makes a sound.*

Robbie What's going on, Mum?

Lynn It's ok, honey.

She gets down on the floor, crouches next to **Joan** *and starts stroking her hair.*

Joan Be careful

Lynn I am careful

Joan Oh . . . /

Lynn It's alright, I'm just stroking your hair, Mum. You like that.

Joan It's magical to see you, Lynn, magical to see you

You loved to play with my hair . . . when you were a little girl.

I must not move /

Re-enter **Hazel**.

Hazel That's right, you mustn't move her because.

We're waiting for the doctor /

Lynn Is that.../

Hazel / yes?

Lynn *(with a tone of reproach)* normal

Hazel Yes

Joan Am I going to be a vegetable like Leon is that what's going to happen / now

Lynn No no, that's not going to happen, Mum

Short silence.

Joan You are my sunshine, yellow was your favourite colour, you wouldn't wear another colour. Do you remember the time we went to picnic . . . the hills and the rain . . .

Lynn yes, Mum . . . why are you thinking of that.

Joan *loses the train of thought.*

Joan I wanted to tell you . . .

Trails off.

Hazel Would you like some water?

Lynn Aren't you, why aren't you watching her I mean she was falling at / home

Hazel we watch her don't you / worry but this isn't the same.

Lynn Sorry but sorry but I don't want her to be alone!

Hazel She's not.

Lynn She's alone, left alone.

Hazel She's not alone, we are here for her, but she's been quite low. And her friend died . . . she saw her a lot.

Lynn *understands that this is directed at her.*

Lynn I just want my mum to be . . . not find her on the floor I mean shit

You / know?

Hazel I'm taking care of her

Lynn she's on the floor, she's been lying here for ages /

Joan Lynn stop

Lynn You know, we really are spending all the money we have and yeh, / well I'm just

Hazel Yeh?

Lynn yes I expect service,/ some service that we are owed

Hazel yes, service, what is owed to you.

She's on the floor! Yes, she's on the floor but do you know why?

I'M SORRY. I don't owe you anything but I AM taking / care of your mother.

Joan STOP STOP! AHH! AHH!

Hazel *steps back, puts her hand over her mouth.*

Hazel I'm sorry I didn't mean that, you know . . .

I'm just exhausted. /

Lynn I'm sorry.

Hazel no everything / is fine

Lynn I JUST WANT to take care of my mum and make sure she's . . . she's ok . . . Sorry.

Robbie yes /

Hazel No I'm sorry. I didn't mean to get angry that wasn't appropriate. I'm fond of your mum.

Joan she is my daughter my only daughter.

Tell Robert we are on the hills, it's raining but we're coming /

Lynn Mum.

Joan It's getting dark but I'm strong I'm strong and I'm walking . . .

Lynn *goes to where the bowl of fruit is that she thinks should be filled. It's not.*

Lynn should there be fruit here? Or?

Hazel No.

Lynn I'll get some /

Hazel OK.

Exit **Hazel**. **Robbie** *takes over the stroking of* **Joan**'*s hair.*

Joan Is Lynn here?

She suddenly wonders where her daughter is.

My little girl, stroke my hair, where are you? I want **Robert**.

Lynn I'm here

Mama, I'm here.

Pause.

Lynn I'm here.

Robbie We're here, Grandma, I'm stroking your hair

He looks at **Lynn** *who looks away.*

Blackout.

Scene Two

The same place.

February.

Hazel *is washing* **Joan**, *who is now totally bedbound. She undoes her night dress so that her chest is able to be washed. She washes her arms, using a sponge in a basin. She lifts her up. And then puts her down and slowly puts her nightdress back on.*

Joan *looks fixedly at something in front of her.* **Hazel** *notices, looks at it, sees nothing, looks at* **Joan** *again.*

Blackout.

Scene Three

The same place.

A few days later.

Laurie *is there. He is thinner, he is dressed slightly differently. Even though he's only been gone a few months, he's changed a lot.*

Laurie Grandma

Grandma

Looking around.

Laurie Grandma, it's me.

Laurie

Joan I was sleeping

OH

Laurie?

Laurie Sorry, yeah, I wanted to come and see you, like sorry

Joan You are

LAURIE

Quiet.

Laurie Yes.

Yeah

I mean

Totally.

I was just a bit.. I don't know. I'm sorry I think I was a bit scared.

Mum really needs you. grandma.

Silence.

Fuck like I heard they said like you slept

I think you slept

Like a day.

Joan I sleep all the time.

I didn't live today because I slept all day.

Cough.

I am entering the last part.

Laurie .

Joan It's strange

Quiet, **Joan** *starts to talk but it is as if she is looking through him somehow. She seems to no longer recognise him.*

That's you Paul?

Laurie no it's me

Joan Laurie . . .

Are we on the hills?

Enter **Lynn** *and* **Hazel** *and* **Robbie.**

Lynn mum

Joan The hills.

I am on a hill. There are people.

Lynn Mum-

Laurie Grandma, it's LAURIE! Fuck! Mum!

Joan *looks at him and it should feel like she is at once looking at him and at Paul.*

Hazel It's okay

It's all good come on now. She's a little delirious.

Lynn MUM.

I'm here mum

Hazel *leaves the family to it.* **Lynn** *has bought some flowers.*

Joan I don't - know

Lynn She can smell them here!

Laurie Mum /

Robbie That's nice, Mum. *Beat.*

Lynn Mama?

In a weak voice, secretive looking above her, where she did before. **Joan** *has suddenly seen something.*

Joan I don't want to see that circle!

Lynn No, Mum

There's nothing there.

Laurie .

Joan .

Are the children here?

Lynn Yes, they're here.

Joan It's winter.

Trails off

Joan The leaves are all gone from my tree.

I never saw any of that before.

Do I need to die now? When do I need to die?

Robbie *runs out.*

Are you going to the hills?

Joan *goes back into a kind of sleep-like state.*

Laurie what is that hills thing.

Lynn Oh it's nothing, it's.

Just one time we went for a Picnic, and we went much higher up that usual . . . and we got stuck in the rain..

As if she's remembering now. But still, throwing the story away, not making it sentimental in anyway.

but, mum took the torch and. . . . She walked us down!

Go and check on Robbie.

Exit **Laurie. Lynn** *looks at her mother.*

And then we drove home and we sang in the car.
Joni Mitchell. And you taught me the words.

Lynn *hums but gets self conscious. It can be funny.*

Lynn Hold my hand, Mum

Hold my hand.

Joan *beams in a smile.*

Joan .

Lynn *feeds* **Joan** *some yoghurt.* **Lynn** *stops the feeding. She's upset for a second. Looks away, ashamed.*

Lynn I've been a terrible daughter, I'm sorry. I wish we'd done more together.

Lynn *dries her tears a bit and looks at her mother, holds her hand. Stares at her for a long time, as her gaze shifts, somehow, away from the world of the living. Here the breath is amplified.*

Joan There's this circle in front of me

Lynn There's nothing mum

Joan get it away from me

Joan *goes back to sleep.*

Lynn *thinks of sitting in bed with her, lying next to her and holding her. She goes to the bed, gets in, but then, just as she's on the bed, she changes her mind. Doesn't dare.*

Joan Ah . . .

Breaking the fourth wall, and here, possibly some of the dead in the audience begin to stand up.

there are people

Lynn Mum?

Joan Get that circle away from me. You're pushing me over the cliff

Pause.

Go away.

Lynn I'm not trying to push you

Joan .

A little silence. During this, **Hazel** *comes in.*

I feel like I'm over a hole

am I

In a green place.

Blackout or another kind of lightning change.

Scene Four

Lights up on **Joan** *gasping, in a kind of rattle. The sound of the breath is amplified, but runs underneath the scene, a kind of intermittent and worrying metronome.* **Joan** *has her mouth open during this.*

A time.

Lynn Why is she gasping like that?

They listen to the gasping.

Hazel It's ok it isn't painful for her

Lynn Can she speak?

Hazel I don't think she can now.

Lynn She won't speak again.

I HAVE to ask her some things!

Hazel *has a sympathetic look.*

When did she last sip? Did she sip

Hazel it wasn't since yesterday when you were here.. but that's ok, it's normal.

Lynn *crouches, her mother is looking at her, breathing loudly, gasping, but then stops.*

Lynn Did she?

Joan *takes a breath.*

Hazel No, no, that's normal, they alternate breaths when..

she's just moving towards the actively dying phase, when the body knows it needs to store oxygen. She's at peace, I think

I'll give you a minute..

Lynn no, oh..

Hazel lingers

Mum? Can you hear me.

Try and smile if you hear me

Did she smile?

haze

They look at her with insistence, trying to make out what she is doing, is she smiling or not.

Hazel Yeh there's a little movement there, in the lip, it's a smile. They can hear everything you know hearing is the last thing to go.

Lynn So I can talk to her?

Mummy?

Mummy I just want to let you know I am so so sorry. And

I really love you.

.

I really hope you're at peace.,

Lynn *adds a blanket to her mother's bed.*

Joan *begins to be agitated. Some kind of sound*

Oh no.. oh no..

Hazel

Hazel it's ok, she's ok.

Hazel pulls the blanket back a bit.

Lynn I don't know what to do mummy

She takes her hands.

Your hands are cold

She touches her feet

Your feet too

Hazel *checks the feet.*

Hazel it's normal, it's just the body slowly going to sleep.

I'll give you a minute, I'll go and check on the boys.

Exit **Hazel, Lynn** *is alone,* **Joan** *continues her breath, she has one eye open,* **Lynn** *crouches so she can see her mother.*

Lynn mummy, it's Lynn..

Joan *tries to make a sound*

I just want you to know we love you, and it's ok you don't need to worry..

We love you

.

Are you trying to say something mummy.

I want you to know..

It's ok.

Are you saying something

Joan *makes a groaning sound and it's very hard to make out what it is. This, despite her best efforts to hold it together, distresses Lynn*

Mummy?

what should I do? How should I live?

She waits for an answer just breathing.

I'm sorry..

Joan, *it is a* **HUGE** *effort for her to speak.. several failed attempts.*

Joan shhhnnn.

Lynn What did you say?

Joan Shiii

Nnn

Lynn Sham, Shame?

Joan Shiiinneee

Lynn .

Shine?

You want me to shine?

Joan .

Shine.

Joan *goes back to the breathing*

There is a moment of peace between them.

Enter **Hazel** *with the children*

Robbie Grandma

As the family approach the bed, **Joan** *gets up, and goes into the audience, into the realm of the dead. She walks gracefully, full of peace.*

Grandma

Laurie Grandma

I'm sorry I

.

I love you.

Hazel Don't worry, she can hear you.

Robbie *gets out his cello, plays a few notes but then is interrupted.*

Lynn Stop playing, darling

One second

Mum

Mum

She turns, as if she feels **Joan's** *presence in the realm of the dead. Suddenly she sees her (in the audience/ dead), understands, walks towards the audience, right to the edge, looks at* **Joan***, sitting in the audience. Straight into her eyes. There is a kind of kindness coming from them, across the divide, between life and death.*

Mummy?

Blackout

Scene Five

The same place.

The next day.

There is less furniture in the room now. **Fanta** *is clearing away the room.* **Hazel** *enters.*

Hazel there's a new /

Fanta Yes

Hazel At 2pm . . .

Looks at her papers.

A Mrs Morris, Susan Morris.

She goes out then pops back.

Thank you, Fanta.

No real reaction from **Fanta**.

Fanta *starts mopping the floor. She begins to sings a joyful pop song that she is listening to through earphones.*

As she is singing, this time the light is on and we are not in blackout, crew come on to dismantle the Care Home and build the family home. There is a large family picture with **Lynn**, *the two children and a man, who we can see clearly, and we understand is* **Leon**.

As the crew busy themselves, we see **Lynn** *walking through the Care Home, carrying a box of* **Joan**'*s stuff. She enters her home as it is being finished around her, seeing the technicians and the change. The theatre is totally visible now. There is a loud piece of music playing, as the worlds blend and the theatre of it all is visible.*

No blackout.

Epilogue

One year after the beginning of the play, March.

Same light – no blackout to mark beginning of the scene.

It is another anniversary of the death of **Leon***. On the table are two urns of ashes.* **Joan***'s and* **Leon***'s.*

They are readying themselves to at last go and spread them in the garden.

Lynn *is now at the front of the stage, amongst the seats spread out in the audience.* **Lynn** *is talking to the audience, one by one, picking out people to speak a sentence to. Now, in the performance, the worlds of the dead and the living are blended.*

Lynn *laughs, lightly.*

Lynn Ah, Leon

You always said I was a . . . mess, that I needed to get things in order . . . oh

Calling up to the kids who are upstairs.

Come on kids, hurry up, it's gonna get dark . . .

Back to audience.

You said, when we met your brother 'she's still finding, exploring, herself, and she can grow'

Robbie *passes by. He's looking for his shoes – doesn't react, is used to the* **Lynn** *talking to herself – goes up the stairs.*

Lynn Oh dear, my love. I can still grow. Mum. I told you.

She then thinks of her mother. Looks at another person.

Laurie *(from upstairs)* Mum!

Lynn I'm living. Yes, I'm living.

Laurie *(from above)* mum stop talking to yourself what the fuck

She hears him, lowers her voice a little.

Lynn I'm proud of myself. You'd be proud, Mum, you'd be proud too.

She looks at the picture of them on the wall.

Laurie *comes down, like* **Robbie** *he is dressed in black as if to go to a ceremony.*

Laurie stop talking to who you're fucking talking to.

Robbie *comes in.*

Very quickly, no breaks:

Robbie Laurie stop yelling at her

Laurie you're mental

Robbie I can't find my shoes

Laurie you're talking to yourself /

Robbie yeah / mum . . .

Laurie you talk to yourself who the fuck are you talking to.

Lynn nobody

Laurie you're lying you're lying stop freaking me out I don't want to hear about the dead and shit let's just do this and fuck that's it but fuck Mum leave it

Lynn no

Robbie I can't find my shoes!

Lynn put on the other ones

Robbie no no I want those!

Lynn I'll fetch them

Robbie they are not in my room!

Lynn *escapes past her son to fetch the shoe already upstairs:*

Lynn yes they are.

Exit upstairs.

Laurie so she wants to go to the woods like now?

Robbie yeah

That's fine.

Laurie don't you mind

Robbie she's mental, who cares

Laurie .

Robbie anyway I'm out of here as soon as I can, like legally.

Laurie what's that got to do with anything?

Robbie I'm moving to Tokyo or maybe Canada. I'll decide when I'm fifteen.

Laurie As if.

Robbie be nice, we're going to the woods like we went with daddy and grandma

Laurie no I don't want to.

Lynn *comes down the stairs.*

Lynn I found them

She gives **Robbie** *the shoes.*

Robbie I'm coming

He puts them on, on the stairs.

Laurie I hear you breathing, crying in your room, talking to yourself laughing, it fucking freaks me out like I just don't want any more of it I'm done

Lynn *says the below with a kind of laughter, a little chuckle almost and nods her head.*

Lynn I cry, I weep because all I could do was laugh but bit by bit, yes I begin to grieve.

Laurie Who the hell are you talking to? not Dad / fuck not to

Lynn no, but yes, no, sometimes . . . I talk to him . . . and to Grandma too

Laurie I'm not going. I'm going up /

Lynn you can't tell me to stop talking to him

Smiling, with feeling and pointing to her heart.

He's there.

Robbie Let's go

Laurie *grabs the urn containing his father's ashes, opens it and throws them at his mum. A cloud of ash covers the stage. He goes towards* **Joan***'s but stops.*

Laurie He's dead! He's fucking dead!!!

Mum

Mum sorry!

Lynn *has the ashes on her and doesn't know what to do with them. She tries to collect them and put them in something or in a pile to keep them. For a short while it's all gestures without words.*

Laurie Mummy Mummy

Lynn *goes to* **Laurie**. *Holds him.*

Suddenly **Laurie** *starts screaming like a wounded animal.*

Laurie WAAAGHHHHH WAAAAGHHH WAAAAGGHHHHH!

Little by little it calms down a bit, **Robbie** *goes up the stairs.*

Lynn Robbie my LOVE

Wait

Robbie he's mental

He starts to pick up the ashes.

Lynn it's ok

Leave it

Leave it all, we'll clean up later. We'll do it later

She looks into the urn.

There's enough left.

Lynn *goes to the bathroom to wash herself. Meanwhile* **Laurie** *picks up some ashes with his hands.*

As he does this, a man rises from the audience, who is the same person as in the family photo: **Leon**, *the father.* **Laurie** *and* **Lynn** *can't see him. He walks down the aisle sits in the front row and watches his son.*

After a moment **Laurie** *goes to the piano and plays a few bars.*

Lynn *speaks from the bathroom.*

Lynn Oh it's just magical when you play.

The lights begin to dim. As he plays, **Leon** *comes up to him, and places his hand on his shoulder. He looks back to* **Joan**, *who also stands.* **Robbie** *comes down the stairs and picks up both* **Joan** *and* **Leon**'s *ashes and holds them in a loving embrace as the darkness falls, slowly, and the family are together, between life and death.*

End of play.